Bishops: Their Status and Function

OTHER BOOKS BY KARL RAHNER

The Eternal Year

Theological Investigations,
Vol. I: God, Christ, Mary and Grace

Theological Investigations,
Vol. II: Man in the Church

Bishops: Their Status and Function

by KARL RAHNER, S.J.

Translated by EDWARD QUINN

A CHALLENGE BOOK
HELICON—BALTIMORE

This is a translation of Über den Episkopat *originally delivered as a lecture, then published in* Stimmen der Zeit *and finally included in* Das Amt der Einheit: Grundlegendes zur Theologie des Bischofsamtes, *a symposium on the basic theology of the episcopal office (Schwabenverlag, Stuttgart, 1964).*

Library of Congress Catalog Card Number—65-15043.

HELICON PRESS INC.

1120 N. Calvert Street

Baltimore, Maryland 21202

©Karl Rahner, 1963

English translation © Burns & Oates Ltd., 1964

MADE AND PRINTED IN THE REPUBLIC OF IRELAND BY CAHILL & CO., LTD., PARKGATE PRINTING WORKS, DUBLIN. NIHIL OBSTAT: JOANNES M. T. BARTON, S.T.D., L.S.S., CENSOR DEPUTATUS; IMPRIMATUR: PATRITIUS CASEY, VICARIUS GENERALIS; WESTMONASTERII: DIE 5A SEPTEMBRIS 1964. THE 'NIHIL OBSTAT' AND 'IMPRIMATUR' ARE A DECLARATION THAT A BOOK OR PAMPHLET IS CONSIDERED TO BE FREE FROM DOCTRINAL OR MORAL ERROR. IT IS NOT IMPLIED THAT THOSE WHO HAVE GRANTED THE 'NIHIL OBSTAT' AND 'IMPRIMATUR' AGREE WITH THE CONTENTS, OPINIONS OR STATEMENTS EXPRESSED.

Contents

THE QUESTIONS AT ISSUE   9

I. BACKGROUND: THE NATURE OF THE CHURCH'S
CONSTITUTIONAL LIFE   13

II. BISHOPS: THEIR STATUS AND FUNCTION   23

  1. The college of cardinals   23
  2. Titular bishops   27
  3. "Relative" and "absolute" ordination   30
  4. The nature of a diocese   34
  5. The bishop and his priests   44
  6. The unity of office and powers in the
     Church   50
  7. Exemption   57
  8. The bishop's functions   62
  9. The concept of the patriarchate   63
  10. An episcopal advisory body to the pope   67

NOTES   73

Abbreviations

CJC = Code of Canon Law (*Codex Juris Canonici*).

DS = *Enchiridion Symbolorum Definitionum et Declarationum de Rebus Fidei et Morum.* Quod primum edidit Henricus Denzinger et quod funditus retractavit, auxit, notulis ornavit Adolfus Schönmetzer, S.J. (Herder, Barcelona, Freiburg/Breisgau, Rome, New York, 1963).

The Questions at Issue

THE question of the episcopate in the Church, of its collegial unity and of its function in the Church as supreme holder of all authority in union with the pope, is one of the foremost of those to be dealt with by the present Council. But, in view of the nature of a Council, the form and scope of the utterances open to it, there is only a little to be said expressly on this theme—although this little is of the greatest and most fundamental importance. We may expect it in the first place to define that there exists in the Church not only an aggregate—an abstract total—of many individual bishops, but a real "college", as a collegial unity (a "moral person"); that this collegially constituted unity of the whole episcopate belongs to the immutable constitutional law of the Church (is of "divine" and not positive, ecclesiastical, variable law); that this college has a head in the Roman Pontiff, who is not merely *princeps inter pares,* but (precisely as head of this college) possesses supreme authority in the sense defined at the First Vatican Council; and that therefore this college is such and can act as such at all times only in union with the pope. Secondly, we may expect the Council to say that the college understood in this way is the holder of the supreme plenitude of authority in the Church (power of orders and of jurisdiction in the three "offices" of teaching, priesthood and episcopal government), which exists in this Church in accordance with the will of Christ and the nature of the Church. It will, we think—thirdly—define that this college exercises its power not only (solemnly) at an Ecumenical Council, but *can* exercise it also outside such a Council (under the conditions for this which flow from its nature, the most important being of course the co-operation of the pope). In the fourth place, from these dogmatic principles there will certainly be drawn some (modest) conclusions: that every bishop has a responsibility (if not jurisdiction) for the whole Church, which has to be exercised as a duty of assistance emerging from the office itself (for example, towards the missions); that episcopal conferences are a practical consequence of this fraternal unity of the bishops with one another.

Presumably, nothing will be said about the exact relationship of the pope to the (remainder of the) college: that is, on the question, expressly left open by the First Vatican Council in regard to the relation between pope and Council and today still disputed, as to whether there are *two* inadequately differentiated subjects of supreme power (pope and college) or only one; this last theory again being open to a great variety of interpretations. Other questions, too, will remain open: *how* did the holder of ecclesiastical authority emerge from the "constitution" of the apostolic, primitive Church? What, in other words, is the *exact* historical derivation of the episcopal from the apostolic college? And, linked with the latter query is the question of the way in which what is ultimately the one office of the Church divided itself into the episcopal office and the office of the simple priest, thus also of the exact delimitation of these two powers. Neither will the Council be able to tell us how exactly the reception of the individual bishop into the college takes place (we shall be speaking of this question shortly). The Council will not discuss the precise modalities of the extra-conciliary but collegial act of the college; which means that we shall not discover from it what types of initiative are open to the college with reference to its head; in what form (express or tacit, canonically established or paracanonical) the co-operation of the pope can or must take place; whether or not what is known as the "ordinary magisterium" of the college of bishops (together with the pope), which—according to Catholic teaching—possesses under certain conditions the same infallibility as a papal definition *ex cathedra*, is such a collegial act (as seems quite obvious to us).

I

Background: The Nature of the Church's Constitutional Life

WE do not intend here either to enter into the theological justification of the teaching put forward by the Council or directly to respond to the questions already mentioned, which remain open and are involved in this teaching. Instead, we shall try—on our own account and at our own risk—to gain from this teaching some insight into the possible practice of the Church in the future. In so far as it is necessary *for this purpose* also to give an opinion on theologically disputed questions, we must naturally attempt to do so. At the same time, we must not overlook the fact that the practical possibilities envisaged *from* the standpoint of such theological opinions may still be possibilities even if the opinions are incorrect. Positive legal ordinances in the Church within the scope of her immutable, divine constitutional law may be justified in a variety of ways: they are not necessarily impossible or inopportune if a particular justification does not command unanimous assent.

In all the reflections which follow one thing must not be forgotten: the Church is an eschatological, redemptive institution, at all times encompassed by the grace of God, and simultaneously a visible community which embodies the historical presence of this redemptive institution in a more or less sacramental fashion (that is, the permanent, effective presence of grace). Thus it comes about that her constitutional structure, in so far as this is of divine institution, shares in her indefectibility. Essential elements, therefore, in what ought to be the Church's constitution simply cannot completely disappear from the life of the Church or be totally overlooked. It cannot, for instance, happen that the college of bishops (under the pope as head), as holder of supreme authority in the Church, should one day be simply ignored or cease to be a factor influencing the life of the Church. And a brief, unprejudiced glance suffices also to observe the reality and effectiveness of such an institution.

Nevertheless, none of this excludes the possibility that much in such realities may be actively existing in a paracanonical fashion. The very fact that there is properly no written constitution of the Church proves this. The Code of Canon Law does not provide it, even though it gives a name to some elements which belong to the constitution. Moreover, the Church's awareness of her constitution has a history, just as much as her dogma and her understanding of faith. As this awareness lives by her continuing, spontaneous life, so it has in its development and history also an influence on the concrete life of the Church. Furthermore, the constantly changing external historical situation of the Church demands a constant renewal of the concrete expressions of her permanent, essential structure, corresponding to the conditions of the particular time, because in fact also the *real* essence of the Church (which is something more than the idea of her essence) always exists in man as contingent and historical and in the Church's historically conditioned action.

Thus it is obvious that the permanent nature of the Church, her divinely bestowed constitution, can emerge with varying degrees of clarity, purity and effectiveness in the historical phenomenon of the Church. In this sense, for instance, the papal primacy of jurisdiction was undoubtedly not always "present" in the same way as it is now. Consequently, we can and must ask ourselves whether one or another element of the Church's constitution might appear in a purer state, might be more intensively lived: whether perhaps the hazards of historical development may not obscure such elements, whether the "phenotype" (if we may use the expression) might not correspond better in constitutional law (in a written or unwritten constitution and in constitutional life) to the "genotype" of the Church in constitutional theology. Doubt as to the obviousness of these possibilities can arise only when we allow the Church's constitution to be reduced to a written document, so that any likelihood of deviation from it or mystery within it would be removed in that it becomes identical with the paragraphs of a constitution formulated in a series of propositions. In such a situation the constitutional life of the Church could be examined solely on the basis of whether or not these paragraphs were being properly observed.

Moreover, in reviewing the earliest development of

the dogma and life of the constitution in the transition from the Church of the Apostles (the "primitive Church", in the theological sense of the term) to the Church of the second century ("early Catholicism"), we must keep in mind the following: In certain circumstances a *development* of the constitution is possible and historically observable, which, while it is really an historical process in which some aspect of the constitutional structure of the Church that in its original form was capable of evolving in a number of different directions has been pruned and refined, nevertheless has and retains for the Catholic conception of the Church the character of divine law. For this purpose, it is necessary only (a) for us to understand that every historically unique structure—and thus also the Church—has in many respects a "one-track" history and therefore not every development and historical decision can or must be revised; (b) for us to be able and allowed to presuppose that such a development (later demonstrable as historically intelligible and justified, if not perhaps as "inevitable") was a legitimate— if not simply necessary—decision, bringing about in an appropriate and inevitable way the concrete realization and specific determination in *one* direction of what was perhaps in itself a plurivalent possibility; and (c) to assume that such a decision was made in apostolic times—that is, it can be regarded as part of the event of revelation and not merely as belonging to the tradition of that revelation, "completed with the death of the last apostle".

If then, for example, at the end of apostolic times,

there is in practice everywhere an episcopal constitution of the Church, as it is historically perceptible everywhere at the beginning of "early Catholicism", this can be understood as of divine institution *without* having to show it as so clearly outlined in the New Testament, so unambiguously predominant over "presbyteral" tendencies, that a different constitutional development would have been utterly *inconceivable* from the very beginning. This observation is not unimportant here. Even though we have neither the duty nor the intention of proving the collegiality of the episcopal college from the *loci theologici* of dogma and canon law, an observation of this kind can still bring out the fact that the constitutional structure of the Church, as it later becomes more clearly evident, is really derived from the New Testament and in what sense this is so: this fact we shall take for granted in the reflections which follow. And, moreover, it is precisely the collegial, the "presbyteral" (if the word is rightly understood) idea in the constitution of the Church for which practical concrete expressions have been here elaborated—without endangering the "monarchical" idea in the same constitution.

We begin our reflections with the question as to how exactly the co-optation of a bishop into the college is related to his appointment as bishop, and this co-optation to the bestowal of his office (by ordination and the grant of jurisdiction or by the former alone). Do these two aspects of the episcopal office (membership of the college: office of bishop) and of the bestowal of office (reception into the college: appointment to office) *mutually* coincide in a reciprocal relationship, or is membership of the college merely a kind of secondary *consequence* of the individual episcopal office and its bestowal?

We can study this question also in the analogous case: is the pope supreme head of the Church simply and solely because he is Bishop of Rome, with whose Roman episcopal office the supreme pastoral office is linked (inseparably or—by a papal act—separably), or is he—at least in reality—with an absolutely logical "simultaneity" or even a logical "priority", head of the whole Church and *so* elected that he *therefore*, or as a result of this, also becomes Bishop of Rome? At a papal election is the successor of Peter chosen in so far as this person is also ultimately supreme pastor of the Church, independently of the Roman episcopal office, so that *thereby* also the Bishop of Rome is appointed, because in fact Peter also ruled over the Roman community? Or is the first aim to elect "only" the Bishop of Rome, who by the fact that he is Bishop of Rome is also the holder of the universal Petrine office, because this must exist in the Church and this supreme pastoral office also pertains to the Bishop of Rome as successor of Peter—who was the first Roman bishop? The practical consequences that may emerge from this tricky and apparently uninteresting question (for the pope and, here above all, for the bishops) will become clear later.

In answering these two questions, which are ultimately one, we are not claiming that there is an absolutely *one*-way real and logical relation of priority or posteriority between the two factors, which are in fact present in each of the two offices (pope and bishop). We shall be satisfied with asserting at least a *reciprocal* relationship between the two factors, that is, to refute the opinion that membership of the college or supreme pastoral office is merely an additional consequence of the other factor (episcopal, mostly territorially limited individual office: Roman-local episcopal office). We are saying, therefore, that we can and must see the existing state of affairs *at least also* in such a way as to be able to state: *because* someone (by consecration and canonical appointment) is accepted into the episcopal college, he is a bishop. *Because* a person is elected as supreme pastor of the Church (and accepts this), he is Bishop of Rome. And not *merely* vice-versa. We know that this thesis, which we have stated so cautiously, does not possess a final formal-juridical and logical clarity. But it seems to us to be justified (at least as a minimal theory) and it suffices for the insight which we are seeking to gain into the existing or desirable practice of the Church.

In order to justify the thesis, we must first of all point out that the episcopal college is regarded in the whole Christian tradition as the successor of the apostolic college. That the bishops are the successors of the apostles in their (inheritable) office is Catholic dogma. If an episcopal college exists and an apostolic college existed, then—assuming this teaching of faith—it can and must be said that the episcopal *college* as such is the successor of the apostolic *college* as such. Otherwise even the authority of a Council simply cannot be explained, since the individual bishop is not infallible,

while the Council is; yet this supreme authority and
infallibility cannot be committed to it by the pope. For
then this *transmitted* authority could not be—as in
fact it is—the supreme power in the Church.

That is why Salaverri, for example, qualifies as
Catholic dogma the thesis that the episcopal college
(within and without the Council) is (in certain conditions) the holder of infallible teaching authority. The
college succeeds as such to the apostolic college and is
formally the continued existence of this: within it, *as*
member, the bishop has the highest authority he can
ever possess. But the apostolic college was not constituted by—if the reader will pardon the expression—
local apostles. Its existence and authority are really
prior to an eventual undertaking of a territorial individual function on the part of the individual apostle—
even if the legendary distribution of the world between
the apostles were true. And likewise there was a time
at least at which originally the Petrine office in Peter
himself and his function as head of the apostolic college was not "locally" specified. Neither Peter nor the
apostolic college properly exercised the function of
"local bishop" of Jerusalem: this was always considered to be vested solely in James.

If then the episcopal college as such is formally the
successor of the apostolic college as such, this characteristic must also belong to it. *As* college it is not simply
the union of *local* bishops as such, but a collegial directive body, which *as* such cannot derive its authority
from the locally restricted authority of its members as
bishops of a particular place. Naturally, the theological

problem as to how this succession-college comes to be constituted by men who (at least for the most part and at first solely) possessed a locally limited ecclesiastical function demands an answer; naturally, it is possible to penetrate from this point onwards more deeply into the *difference*—which also exists—between apostolic college and episcopal college. But these questions, which are not to be discussed here, must not be allowed to obscure the fact that the episcopal college as such derives its existence and its right from a college which did not consist of men with a territorially circumscribed mission and authority and in any event cannot formally be made up of individual bishops *in so far as* they have territorially limited powers.

This holds also for the Petrine office. The function of supreme pastor cannot be derived from the local function of Peter and his successors *as* holders of these local offices and powers. That the early Church was aware of this basic structure is evident from the practice of choosing a new local bishop, not only by the people and clergy of that place, but with the co-operation of neighbouring bishops, metropolitans and patriarchs. The election of the pope by the college of cardinals is—formally, at least—a choice by the suburbicarian bishops, or at any rate not simply by the representatives of the Roman community as such. That there also exists an *international* college of cardinals, which seems to us now almost self-evident, shows that today at least it is a question formally and immediately of the election not only of the Roman Bishop as such, but of the supreme pastor of the whole Church. That is precisely why the college of cardinals has been increasingly internationalized since the establishment of this mode of election. The assignment of a Roman titular church to those cardinals who are not suburbicarian bishops clearly confirms that no one has even doubted or wished to obscure the fact that the appointment of a Roman local bishop was also involved.

As a result of these indications, we may certainly say: acceptance into and membership of the episcopal college (likewise the appointment of the supreme pastor *as* such) is an essential aspect of the episcopal (Petrine) office, ranking equally with this and directly implied in it or in its bestowal; and it may not be derived one-sidedly *from* the other aspect (local authority) or seen merely from that aspect. A bishop is bishop of a place because and *in so far as* he belongs to the supreme directive body of the Church, even though this does not mean that the justification of the opposite view is to be disputed. Consecration and canonical mission have *also* immediately the meaning of acceptance into this college, which does not itself possess a territorial character and does not gain its authority over the whole Church through the individual bishops piecing together their territorially limited powers and thus covering with this the whole earth. Nevertheless, the fact remains—and it is important—that they represent in the college their particular Churches and place at the disposal of the whole Church the treasures of each of these: spiritual character, historical situation, vital force, and the will to accept responsibility for the whole of the Church.

II

Bishops: Their Status and Function

FROM the point thus reached, we must try to gain that insight into certain practical problems of which we spoke. We shall not attempt to deal with these systematically.

1. *The college of cardinals*

If the college of bishops with the pope as its head possesses the supreme plenitude of authority in the Church, it seems self-evident that the same body should be responsible for electing the head when this becomes necessary. For—if we are right—the appointment of the pope as supreme pastor of the whole Church is *dogmatically* at least as important as the election of the pope as Bishop of Rome. And the first standpoint is today *in practice*, in contrast to the first centuries of the Church, of so much greater importance than the second that in any kind of dispute about "competence" in regard to the method of election it must have preference.

An election of this kind, by the body which represents the whole Church, impossible in the first eighteen hundred years of Church history, would today, because of the ease of modern travel and communication, be quite practicable. We have already said that the historical development of the college of cardinals was itself implicit in the understanding that it was not a question merely of the election of the Bishop of Rome, but of the choice of a man in whom the whole Church as such may and must be interested. Thus a purely systematic reflection would naturally lead to the conclusion that those who represent the whole Church must choose its head. Even if we were to say that the immediate assistants of the dead pope are the best elective body, we would once again have to assert: the immediate assistants of the pope in governing the whole Church, from the theological standpoint, are precisely the bishops and not the leaders of the central congregations; these as such have at best an authority over the Church delegated by the pope and not that authority which belongs *jure divino* to the college of bishops.

With all respect, we must once more examine the history and existence of the college of cardinals as the elective body. And we must not lose sight of the fact that, while a papal election by the episcopal college is technically possible today, it would for various reasons be difficult to carry out. Such an election would be practically possible, in fact, only if the assembly of all the bishops were again to form a kind of election-committee (at least preparatory). And thus we should come back precisely to something like a college of cardinals. To give effect to the principle of constitutional theology, that the episcopal college has the prior right of electing the pope, it would be best therefore so to shape the college of cardinals that it could be regarded in practice as the executive of the episcopal college (which does not mean, however, that it is tied to any sort of "mandate" in electing the pope and that a cardinal cannot and must not vote wholly in accordance with his own conscience). As the procedure of the Council has shown, such a representative function of the college of cardinals has in fact been gradually, more or less spontaneously and paracanonically emerging: the cardinals have greater and more extensive voting rights, so that in practice their word in the assembly has more weight than that of other bishops. And yet they speak as members of the episcopal college. The constantly increasing internationalization of the college of cardinals over the past half-century points in the same direction.

In this connection, it is interesting to note that John XXIII consecrated as bishops all the cardinals in curia who were not yet bishops. Apart from emphasizing the dignity and importance of a cardinal, it would be difficult to say what exactly was intended by this. Nor can we yet say whether the practice will be maintained in the future. We may also note that it made one thing remarkably clear: we might have had the impression that the highest grade of the hierarchy was being used almost like titles and orders for more or less social-decorative purposes, that a person received the title of an office which he was never intended to exercise— since as mere cardinals, without being bishops, they would not necessarily *jure divino* have a place and voice at the Council as residential bishops have. In the perspective now opened to us, the matter looks quite different.

It is first of all absolutely appropriate that a man with the rank of cardinal should belong to the episcopal college, since this of its nature (with the sum-total of local bishops having as such equal rank) as the supreme collegial directive body of the Church does not have to consist *merely* of local bishops, but also and rightly includes members who contribute directly to the whole government of the Church as much as do local bishops. And such are the cardinals. To bring these men, too, into the divinely appointed governing college of the Church is, then, properly an adjustment, a simplification and a clarification of her concrete structure: one is doing no more than sacramentally sealing what they are anyway in law and practice. This will remain obscure only as long as we hold the unqualified opinion that the episcopal college must of its nature, in itself and in the first instance, be made up solely of local bishops. If we can overcome this prejudice and see that anyone who really does in fact participate in the supreme governing body of the Church ought also to have the *sacramental* authorization and grace of office for this, then we shall see how realistic was the action of John XXIII. But then the college of cardinals becomes a kind of committee or executive of the episcopal college, to which the election of the pope most appropriately belongs as a result of the ultimate constitutional structure of the Church; and it is also possible to understand why both at present and in the future it is, and will be, best suited to form the papal elective college.

The sole condition is that it should be so made up as truly to represent the whole episcopate. We can now see that it clearly does *not* need to be made up *solely* of archbishops and bishops who rule over a diocese. It is utterly right that men who really count in the central government of the Church (appropriately endowed with the episcopal office) should also be represented there. But if the college of cardinals is seen in this way, we might well say that the dignity of the cardinalate must not be used as a kind of reward and conclusion of a career in the diplomatic or curial service of the Holy See; its bestowal might even be restricted to the time at which a person is effectively engaged in the government of the Church.

2. *Titular bishops*

If the absolutely original nature of the episcopal college admits the possibility of members within it who are not properly local, ruling bishops (or coadjutors of these with the right of succession), then it is conceivable also in principle—because of an obvious realization of the basic constitutional structure of the Church and not only because of the possibility of an "absolute" sacramental ordination—that there are bishops who do not govern any existing diocese, titular bishops of the most varied kind. From our point of view of course the condition of such a possibility—not only as absolutely possible, but as truly homogeneous with the basic constitution of the Church—is that these men clothe an *office*, exercise in the Church a function corresponding to the office of a local bishop, and thus make it appear to be apt and suitable for its holder also to be a member of the supreme governing college of the Church.

There are such functions and offices in the Church. It is impossible to organize the Church *merely* on a territorial basis (even leaving aside the question of her head). The territorial principle is *one* of the important, natural and constant structural principles in a Church made up of human beings conditioned by space and time. But it is not *the* unique structural principle. As there rightly are and must be (we shall have more to say of this later) exempt orders, personal parishes, institutions in the Church, which cut right across the territorial members of the Church or cover several dioceses, so there are offices and functions in the Church of an institutional character which do not fit into a normal, territorial organization of the Church and yet have objectively the same importance for the Church as the function of a local bishop. A Catholic university—for example, of the standing of Louvain— is at least as important a "member" of the Church as a small Italian country diocese. It is therefore not at all irrelevant or alien to the constitution of the Church that its rector should be a bishop. And this holds even though it is quite clear that the episcopal college also in the future will consist and must consist mainly of local bishops, precisely because the great majority of the really significant collective members of the Church will still be territorially distinct dioceses. From this point of view, we might ask frankly whether it would not be most appropriate and in accordance with a clear and bold theology of the Church's constitution if the supreme and permanent heads of the great exempt orders (or of large sections of these) were to become bishops. They do in fact take part in the Council, with voting rights (although this can only be through great, purely historically conditioned distortions of the situation).[1]

Thence also the difference in the constitutional theological significance of the various types of auxiliary bishop may become clear. In accordance with Catholic dogma, the practice of the Eastern Church and certain special regulations of the Latin Church, even a simple priest is sacramentally authorized (with the necessary permission—express or legally established by custom) to administer Confirmation validly and lawfully. In principle, there is nothing against the extension of this practice, particularly as the religious (sacramental, but also psychological and instructive) effect of this sacrament administered by a bishop is no greater than it is through the ministry of a simple priest; the Western practice, moreover, takes up a great deal of a bishop's time which could be better spent on the salvation of souls.[2] Looking at it in this way, we might say that the function of an auxiliary bishop in so far as this consists in Confirmation scarcely endows him with such importance in the Church that he must—*merely for this reason*—be a member of the apostolic episcopal college and therefore a bishop. It is quite right, therefore, from the standpoint of constitutional theology, that the office of a merely auxiliary bishop should be comparatively rare outside Central Europe. On the other hand, in a large diocese which for a variety of reasons—for example, in a large city—cannot conveniently be divided, a second bishop[3] may have so many functions and be so important even beyond his own diocese for the whole Church that—in accordance with the realities of the situation—he likewise ought to be a member of the episcopal college (and therefore is quite rightly a bishop); more so indeed than the bishop of a tiny diocese which might easily be united with its neighbour. Constitutional theology also shows that such auxiliaries are rightly bishops. We have already pointed out that the same might be said, for the same reasons, analogously of really important offices with decisive weight in the central government of the Church. Here too, from the standpoint of our basic conception, conferment of episcopal office may be seen to be not only utterly right, but also positively desirable, even when the holder is not already a cardinal. On the other hand, precisely from the same standpoint, it must be said that episcopal ordination and rank are not suitable as honours to be conferred on the holders of comparatively secondary curial or diplomatic offices or as a means of giving these greater authority in relation to local bishops, particularly if they are themselves subject to superiors who are also bishops or cardinals.

3. *"Relative" and "absolute" ordination*

The meaning of this catchword may be taken as known: in relative ordination a bishop is consecrated as the local bishop of a particular Church; in absolute ordination there is no such reference (and, to remind us that in itself relative ordination is the normal thing, the person is given a titular see *in partibus infidelium*, for which almost two thousand titles are available). This is not the place to recount the reasons for and the misgivings about absolute ordination, which gradually emerged in the course of history alongside relative ordination—regarded for more than a thousand years as the only justifiable form of ordination. But, particularly in the two previous sections, we have presumably obtained the material which will help to clarify further the question of principle. If the episcopal college is one and as such has a function in the Church, and if consecration as such brings the person directly into the college, then constitutional *theology* cannot recognize any purely "absolute" ordination in the straightforward sense of the word: in every ordination in addition to the sacramental power of order, there will be granted membership of the episcopal college—which is the holder, not only of the power of order, but irrevocably of pastoral authority. Every ordination therefore is the grant of a share in the power of the Church in every respect, even though first of all in regard to pastoral authority it comes solely through and in membership of the episcopal college.

To this there corresponds—even apart from our point of view—the theory now beginning more and more to prevail that ordination itself confers a radical, sacramentally based and imprinted capacity for the exercise of pastoral authority, which also finds expression in most liturgies of consecration of the different Churches. If relative ordination exists in a truly

31

theological sense, when there is granted, together with a real office (for example, precisely the function of a member of the college), episcopal participation in the whole power of the Church, then there cannot be any completely absolute ordination. What we call relative ordination in popular or *merely* canonical language is then a particular species of relative ordination: namely, that in which also the office of a *local* bishop is conferred. But that does not alter the theological structure of the conferment of office. Ordination is in both cases "referred"—"relative"—to an office. This theory naturally presupposes that titular bishops also belong to the episcopal college.

Against *this* opinion there can be no serious objection. Such an objection would be justified only if it could be proved that someone with power of jurisdiction in his own see could alone be a member of the institution holding supreme power of jurisdiction in the Church. But such an idea presupposes that the individual bishops in some way pool their territorially and objectively limited powers of jurisdiction and *thus* make up together the supreme holder of the *plenitude* of power of jurisdiction. That this is impossible can be seen most clearly in an office which emerges from this power, the infallible teaching office of this college (together with the pope): a sum of authentic but not infallible teaching authority in the individual bishops does not result in that teaching office which is indefectible both inside and outside the Council. And if it is claimed that this quality of indefectibility on the part of the episcopate as a whole is derived from the infallibility of the pope, then again it is difficult to see how the pope could allow a bishop to share in this only on the condition of his also ruling over a diocese.

This reasoning cannot be refuted by pointing to the fact that titular bishops can be and are indeed members of the Council, but do not *necessarily* have to be such —as they would if they were members of the college. For even if we assume that they are such, it always remains open to positive canon law and to the Holy See, after laying down precisely the positive constitutional law of a Council, for good reasons *not* to call individual members of the episcopal college to it, since as the representative assembly (*as* such *juris humani*) of the episcopal college it does not require a physically complete attendance of all the bishops; and a certain variety in the membership of the college among local ordinaries and *some* kinds of titular bishops need not be questioned. There can really be no doubt that titular bishops also belong to the episcopal college, whether we appeal to general principles or simply to the fact that being a bishop means formally being a member of the college. That would still hold even if we were to insist that there can be various grades and forms of membership in a college and that therefore a titular bishop does not need to be and indeed is not a member of the episcopal college in precisely the same way as a local bishop.[4]

But in addition to this, we can see that the ideal of relative ordination renders it desirable that the subject of ecclesiastical power and dignity should be someone whose *remaining* episcopal function (as distinct from his function as a member of the college) makes him particularly suitable to be a member of the supreme directive body of the Church. Now we have been trying to show on the one hand that there are also such functions, which are not identical with the functions of the local ordinary, and that on the other hand titular bishops quite often exercise functions which of their nature make their holders really seem not to be suitable for membership of the supreme directive body of the Church. A relative ordination desirable in every respect—that is, in constitutional theology and law—would then be that through which a person receives an office or an office is sacramentally consecrated which really qualifies him as a suitable member of the episcopal college. This office may be of local or non-local character. An ordination of purely "absolute" (even if relative in the ordinary sense) and undesirable form would be a consecration which confers nothing more than membership of the college and the simple power of orders, and neither finds already present nor produces in its holder a function making him in his importance for the whole Church "homologous" to a local ordinary.

4. *The nature of a diocese*

If we look to the definitions of the schools of the nature of a diocese, we shall not receive very illuminating answers. A diocese is a member-Church, presided over by a bishop with pastoral authority defined and exactly delimited (in relation to the pope and, if necessary, to patriarch and metropolitan) in canon law. But a bishop (apart from his power of order, which does not indicate any immediately perceptible relation to a delimited territory, or at least in regard to its size and shape) is a man who rules over a diocese with pastoral authority. The circle is complete.

Now, however, as a result of the newly emergent and pressing question in practical canon law and pastoral theology, as to how large a diocese really ought to be, whether dioceses ought to be divided or united, we see that these answers are inadequate. On the other hand, the practical questions mentioned are just those which cannot be answered simply "from the practical point of view". We must first know *what* a diocese ought to be, what really are its functions and what are not, because they can be performed, for example, simply by a dean (empowered under certain circumstances to confirm), or because in any event they can be undertaken only by a "superior bishop", that is, by the metropolitan, the patriarch, or an association of these (or by national or continental episcopal conferences): only then can we ask *how* "in practice" a diocese must be formed in regard to size, institutions, and so on, in order to be able to do justice to these functions. If someone thinks, for instance, that a bishop must "know" all his priests or must himself be able to confirm all who are under his pastoral care, his picture of the ideal size of a diocese will be different from that of a person who rejects such a criterion as too romantic and paternal.

It is of course clear from the beginning that there cannot be an "ideal" picture of the diocese which holds equally for *all* times; nor can a *contemporary* conceptual pattern of the diocese be developed in such a form that we can deduce from it—for example—a certain number of square miles or of inhabitants as the "ideal" size of a diocese today. The former is impossible, because a diocese obviously has in its concrete, historical form very many natural (geographical, racial, social, historical) conditions which are variable. The latter is impossible, because the variations exist simultaneously also today. But, from the basic idea of our reflections, it is certainly possible to say a little about what the diocese might be in the concrete. More anyway than could be derived from the definition with which we began.

It is a good thing at this point once again to "wonder" at the fact that the supreme directive body in the Church—which originally had its normal seat in *one* place, Jerusalem—now consists mainly of men who are simultaneously leaders of a "province" of the Church and are thus "dispersed" throughout the world. This is indeed rarely the case with other sociological structures: the "government", the "council of ministers", of a country will scarcely consist of the leaders of all its provinces. Nor do we cease to wonder when it is simply pointed out that the Roman Pontiff represents the unity of the Church in this directive body, the bishops the plurality and manifold character of her members and therefore come from the whole world. For even if the polar structure of the supreme directive body (a head of the college, able to act personally—synodal plurality of members) includes representatives of the whole Church, their total does not on that account need to be the same as the whole number of the rulers of the local Churches. And yet this by no means self-evident situation is the fact. Again, this is not the place to draw conclusions for the peculiar theological character of the episcopal college and the exact nature of its derivation from the apostolic college on the basis of our observation of the difference between a supra-local apostolic college, which exists in one place, and a college consisting of local bishops, which is "dispersed". (Evidently, this is not the succession-college in the sense that the same permanent college as a moral person is carried on only through other physical persons; but *one* college follows *another* college.)

If we want to appreciate fully this amazing fact, we shall have to say: the members of the supreme directive body of the Church as a whole must be men who administer a part of the Church so considerable in itself that it can rightly expect to have a personal representation in that body. But this means, on the other hand: a diocese must be such (in size, life, character) that in it (precisely in its geographical, historical and religious character at any particular time) the whole of the Church can be seen; that the see can really be designated a "Church", that is, it can be described in the same theological terms (and not merely in those which refer to a part, a province, etc., of the Church) as the Church herself in her entirety—a description which cannot and ought not to be applied in the strict sense, for instance, to a parish.

The Church alone, in fact, in contrast to all other

societies, has this unique characteristic that she can appear as a microcosm of herself in any one place. A particular place in a country is neither more nor less, in these terms, than one of the places belonging to that country: it is a city, a province, which can never rightly be given the same name as the whole country or state. But in the Church it is different: she can be in a place in her entirety and therefore the local community can rightly be called a Church. The Church is present in that place, because her greatest self-fulfilment, which belongs to her as a whole, and which cannot be conceived as greater and more complete in her whole territorial extent, can occur at a particular place and not solely in that whole territorial extent: the celebration of the Eucharist, in which our Lord truly as Lord and sacrifice of the Church is present; the preaching of the operative word of God, in which God's mighty deed for men is effectively proclaimed.

We might conclude from this that, not only the diocese, but simply any localized altar-community is the Church (this difficulty could scarcely be felt in antiquity, since on the whole the really full altar-community still coincided with the community over which the bishop presided). But precisely from this point of view of the local community as a kind of actual presence of the whole Church, we can see that only the community in which the *whole* course of the Church's life—not merely the celebration of the Eucharist (sacrament) and the preaching of the word—can be represented, is really the Church in its entirety, that is, a diocese. Naturally, the reality of this "entirety" is not so conceived as if the Church really existed *in the fullness* of her life wherever there are "genuine" dioceses : what is meant is that a genuine diocese must also be the holder to a sufficient extent of such functions—in addition to the Eucharist and the preaching of the word— as necessarily belong to the whole Church (a requirement varying with times and situations). For only such a constituent part of the Church can claim appropriately that its leader ought to belong to her supreme directive body.

In this respect we must bear in mind that the possibility of the Church as such appearing in some sense as a whole in the world, at a particular point of space and time, depends to a large extent on the secular sociological conditions prevailing at the particular time and in the actual place. In order that a diocese *today* can be a diocese—that is, a Church which truly epitomizes at least in some fashion *the* Church, in all her dimensions —it needs sociological, economic and cultural conditions which simply cannot exist in a very small diocese (we are speaking of a diocese already developed or at least capable of development). What intellectual, cultural and social life is today, its analogue—the Church organized in her theological, intellectual and religious life—must be: this can exist only in relatively large or thickly populated areas. A "village" cannot present the form of a developed, complete diocese. But the same holds also of the small areas which, if we compare them to the earlier social organization, count today as no more than a village. If we want to think of a diocese corresponding to the needs of the present time, we must remember that the basic spatial unit of the local community today is no longer the town, but the industrial area. Just as there was a very gradual historical transition from the village culture to the city, so today we are witnessing a transition from the city-culture to a culture of which the local unit has still to be defined and which we can provisionally describe as the "industrial area". These sociological developments must not be overlooked if we want to discover the nature of a diocese which will be "right" for the present time. The Ruhr district, for instance, is now one diocese.* If such an industrial landscape becomes more and more the normal pattern of human life, what is the consequence for the right size of a diocese?

What we have said up to now may still be a rather vague account of the constitutional theological nature of a diocese: to attempt to make a more direct and precise statement would raise the difficult question—which cannot be dealt with here—of the sense in which the bishop and his see are of divine law; and this again leads to the question as to how and why the one office of the Church (existing and maintained in a succession-college which bears the character of the apostolic college in its unity of the Petrine office and the "twelve") is held by a *territorially* organized college and why—for example—the sum-total of patriarchs or metropolitans alone do not count (*de facto* or *de jure?*) as such a succession-college, so that they would have to be called properly "bishops" in the theological

* Essen. Anticipating Professor Rahner's suggestions the diocese was formed as a single unit in 1957 (Tr.).

sense and what we today call bishops would be in relation to these merely a kind of "superior parish priest" or "dean".[5]

But even this rather vague information as to what a bishop is (as member of the college) and therefore ought to be (in his special office), provides a critical standard in regard to actual dioceses. If a see is expected to represent truly the life of the Church as a whole (in its natural and redemptive-historical character), then this does not exclude, but in fact includes the need of this representation and therefore the form of the diocese to be subject to historical transformation. The ancient local see and the contemporary provincial see (apart from Italy) correspond to the transformation from the ancient city-state (which had also an historical importance in the Hellenistic-Roman Empire) to the nation-state. We cannot enter here into this manifold and—in the individual countries and continents—very varied history of the form and function of a see.

But if our basic premiss is right, certain practical conclusions follow which are by no means irrelevant at the present time. The diocese of today must not be too small, and it must be so constructed as to be capable of effectively exercising the functions (apart from the central government) which belong anyway to the Church. And since the apparatus of the institutional element in the life of the Church in this age of technology and the mass-society necessarily grows more and more complicated (pastoral institutes, training centres for all kinds of church-workers, finance, widely organized charitable activities and much more), the right trend, in view of these facts, is rather to increase than to reduce the size of dioceses. If the large city becomes more and more the normal residential centre, and as in it there is generally only one see, then the large see will inevitably become the normal type of the diocese. This is also theologically justified: the holder of a tiny see of a few thousand souls, particularly in areas where dioceses could easily be amalgamated, has no appropriate claim to be a member of the supreme directive college of the whole Church.[6] This is particularly important at a time when the universal Church has 400 million members and thus almost inevitably 2,000–3,000 bishops, whose number cannot be indefinitely increased if they are really themselves still to form the supreme government of the Church (consider, above all, the technical problems presented by the convocation of a Council).

There is no point in resisting the trend towards relatively large dioceses, in hindering the amalgamation of small sees or in pleading for a division of dioceses for reasons which are mainly of a romantic or paternalist character: the result of such a procedure would be to make only the higher ranking bishops—patriarchs, metropolitans, presidents of episcopal conferences—in practice, if not in name, what bishops ought to be if they are members of the episcopal college; others might still be called bishops, but in reality would not be completely such, being practically merely deans with authority to confirm. They would no longer have the direction of such institutions as make a territorial district into a "Church"

When a diocese cannot by itself support a seminary corresponding to the needs of the present time, when it can no longer support the institutional forms of education and of charitable works, exercise an influence on public opinion, manipulate mass-media, organize intellectual life in such a way that it is all in some sense representative of the whole Church, then it is in fact not a member-Church which ought to be and can be governed by a successor of the apostles, who should have above himself in his normal activity none except the principle of unity in the college, the successor of Peter. In other words, it would be a see in name more than in reality.

If a genuine, large and vigorous see really needs, between its head and the individual local communities, further intermediate authorities with power to act on behalf of, and under the jurisdiction of the bishop—as may well be the case—then, if those available (deans, directors of super-parochial organizations, personal parish-priests—for example, of student-communities —and so on) are numerically inadequate for the purpose, more ought to be created; alternatively, those available should be granted more powers, in accordance with the principle of subsidiary function—which holds also for the Church. But that is not a reason for making dioceses so small that their rulers must sink mentally, sociologically and even in a real sense ecclesiastically, to the level of a parish priest who confirms and has the power to ordain priests. In his pastoral authority also the bishop must be allowed the stature and impact of a successor of the apostles and a member of the government of the Church as a whole. For this there is needed not only the existence of formal pastoral authority: it must also have an object, a field of activity, material suited to its importance on which to work. Naturally, what has been said is meant primarily of a diocese that is fully established, not of one still in the process of construction, the shape and content of which will vary greatly with the variations of time and place and cultural and social progress.

5. *The bishop and his priests*

Here and there some anxiety has been felt about the consequences of marking out more clearly the mission and authority of the bishop as one who rules his diocese in the name of Christ and not merely as an official of the pope. In place of a Roman-centralist (supposedly or really) autocratic government, may there not be a danger of "episcopalism" appearing in practice and an autocratic diocesan government? In Central Europe this does not appear to be a great or pressing danger. The conditions of the diaspora make it remote; bishops and priests, faced by the threat of the new paganism, are too much dependent on one another; if we leave aside a bishop's uncertainties of mood and temperamental outbursts—which can work out well or badly in *any* system, must be borne with patience and good humour, and can always be kept in check if priests have the spirit of brotherhood and are manly and straightforward in dealing with their bishop—then there is no need to fear the emergence of episcopal autocrats. But the problem might arise in other countries with different historical and psychological backgrounds. An African bishop might unconsciously adopt the style of a tribal prince; in one French bishop or another there could be signs of the mentality—so to speak—of the *ancien régime*. To check the danger anywhere it is important to have a lively appreciation of the theologically correct relationship between bishop and priests.

This relationship can be made clear from our starting-point. But this does not mean at all that the relationship between pope and episcopate as defined in constitutional theology is continued downwards absolutely in the same sense and as likewise *juris divini*, that it may therefore be simply transferred with the same meaning and automatically to the relationship between bishop and presbyterium.* Nevertheless, two points may be made. Firstly: the constitutional-theological structure of the Church, in so far as it requires a polar unity of a monarchical and a collegial element in an indissoluble relationship to one another (without therefore being a college consisting simply of equals, as in Ulpian's definition of a college), can still stand as a model of the relationship between bishop and presbyterium. Secondly: if the principle of collegiality in the sense here emphasized is applied at least as a model to this relationship, then it must be said that

* If only the term were not so generally used for "priest's house", "presbytery" would be the obvious translation here. But since Professor Rahner makes a German word and Spicq (*Les Epitres Pastorales*, Paris, 1947) a French word of *presbyterium*, we may be allowed to anglicize it (Tr.).

the priest as a result of his ordination enters into a college, into the presbyterium; his ordination, rightly and fully understood, is an acceptance into this presbyterium which itself must be considered fundamentally as *jure divino*[7] the college for the bishop.

In fact, the New Testament and the early Church do not really take account of the individual priest, but of the presbyterium. This is even united locally with the bishop: it is not merely the sum-total of parish-priests of places where there does not happen to be a bishop, but precisely the college in the place where the bishop is; he does not ordain priests because he cannot himself be everywhere, he ordains someone to assist him in his functions where he is. He does not ordain an individual, but surrounds himself with a college. He does nothing without the presbyterium. This does not mean that he is juridically dependent on or chargeable to his presbyterium, but that he does not think of himself as a lonely autocratic monarch, able or wanting to say: "The bishopric, that am I". We can safely say: "The 'synod' of the bishop with his presbyterium is just as ancient and original (even though it is not on that account of the same kind in constitutional law), as the synods of bishops with one another."

For practical reasons (apart from the rare case of a diocesan synod as provided for in CJC 356–362), it may be legitimate today for the function of the ancient episcopal presbyterium to be largely taken over by the Cathedral Chapter and the rest of the priest-members of the episcopal curia; and in the concrete, in view of the large dioceses necessary today and the local separation of most of the priests from the episcopal centre, this must be done. But if we look at this episcopal curia, keeping in mind the polarity of bishop and presbyterium, we shall have to say: the constitutional-theological structure of the Church is realized purely and clearly when the curia is so selected and so organized that it can really count as the representative of the presbyterium; that is, it is characterized by a relationship in the theological sense such as we have already seen to be desirable as between the college of cardinals and the college of bishops. This does not mean at all that the episcopal curia must be chosen by the presbyterium "from below" (still less act as an organ by which the presbyterium controls the bishop). That is not the case even with the college of cardinals and it would be an infringement of the bishop's authority over the presbyterium. But for constitutional-theological (and not merely pure pragmatic-psychological) reasons, this can certainly mean that the bishop has the moral obligation of so organizing his curia as to make it also the representative body of his presbyterium, which he did indeed ordain as *his* presbyterium, as his council of "elders", even though the observance of this moral obligation is not subject to a legal control on the part of the presbyterium.

It is only when we see the priest always as a member of the presbyterium that we can really understand (particularly when we think of the practice of the ancient Church, with its many small episcopal sees) why not every leader of a firmly established local altar-community of some size—that is, a parish priest above all—is *ipso facto* a bishop. We can then understand why a see is a truly theological institution: not merely an administrative organization of many local communities, but a really spiritual institution. The bishop does not ordain priests in order to send them *away* from him, so that the individual priest exists as such in isolation; but to the members of the presbyterium permanently belonging to him he hands over local, individual tasks and thus remains the episcopal father of his whole diocese.

Hence we can understand also that the local parish is indeed the normal and most frequent type of mission held by a member of the episcopal presbyterium, but that members of the presbyterium as the bishop's representatives might just as well be appointed for other forms of altar-community, if and in so far as such a non-parochial, permanent altar-community (personal parish, monastic community, etc.) is appropriate. The territorial principle is not the sole structural principle. Precisely when the individual priest is seen from the beginning as a member of the presbyterium, it becomes possible to avoid a romantic parochialism which would make the parish priest into a lesser bishop (claiming for him, for instance, irremovability or irreplaceability in the same sense as for the bishop). The dignity of the parish priest is not diminished, but elevated, if he is seen as a member of the episcopal presbyterium, as the representative on the spot of the bishop's Church. But the parish is not a diocese in microcosm. If it were so regarded, it would really also have to become a see. But against such a procedure could be raised all the objections which have just been mentioned with regard to small dioceses.

From the foregoing it at last becomes theologically comprehensible how it is that to this very day the Church's understanding of the faith with regard to the line of division between the sacramental powers of the bishop and those of the priest has never found a final definition. All that can be said with some degree of certainty is that a priest cannot ordain a bishop. It is not, however, certain that he cannot—under certain conditions—validly confer ordination to the priesthood. He can certainly confirm. This is noteworthy. For, since a simple priest can be the holder of all the bishop's powers of jurisdiction, in the abstract, in the light of contemporary theology, it could be conceived that simple priests alone without bishops might administer all the ecclesiastical offices necessary for the life of the Church. Episcopal consecration is a requirement only when bishops are needed; but they are not needed if all their functions, so far as these are necessary for salvation, can be supplied also by simple priests.

These speculations are intended merely to show that the division assigned by divine law between priest and bishop is not so easy to establish as we sometimes think. But this very fact becomes intelligible when we see that the bishop cannot really be thought of without his presbyterium and can therefore be represented—in certain conditions—even by a subordinate member (made such by sacramental ordination) of this union of bishop and presbyterium. This occurs anyway on the most

D

decisive occasion: the celebration of the Eucharist. And since this always has been and is also today the most important function of the bishop (because here in her most intimate mystery the Church becomes wholly, immediately and in the most intensive fashion present in space and time), St Thomas Aquinas and all the great theologians of the Middle Ages made no attempt to distinguish between the sacramentality of episcopal and priestly ordination. Again a portent for what concerns us here: bishop and priest are intimately associated with one another, because the priest is not a smaller "repetition" of the bishop, but a member of his presbyterium, without which in the last resort[8] he cannot be conceived; and *therefore* the priest's authority as representative of the head of the presbyterium is possibly variable and quite probably often did vary at different times in the course of the Church's history, with her varying intention in regard to priestly ordination.[9]

6. *The unity of office and powers in the Church*

Our theme here is the unity, not of the *holders* of offices and powers, but of the offices and powers themselves, in so far of course as this unity can be seen from the unity of the episcopal college with, under—and also through (DS 3051)—the pope and from the indissoluble unity between the bestowal of authority on the bishop and his acceptance into the college. It is obvious that these brief reflections from a particular standpoint do not claim to be a complete treatment of the theme suggested by the catchword "unity of powers".

We start out again from the basic fact that the episcopal college with the pope as its head is the holder of the supreme plenitude of authority in the Church. A society ("people of God", "covenant", "community" of Christ) which proclaims its unity as one of its most essential features, and has *one* aim and *one* function, must necessarily be one also in its office: this ultimately one power and this ultimately one office belong to the episcopal college, in such a way that this is characterized precisely by the full possession of this one authority and this one office. If and in so far as offices and powers, therefore, can and must still be distinguished—for whatever reasons—in this one office and the authority holding it, they cannot simply be added up, but must be grasped in their unity: they must be developed from the basic nature of the Church, her unity, and the unity of her function and aim.

The next step is the observation (partly empirical) that the supreme holder of this one office—that is, the members of this college which is the holder—as such is established in it on the one hand by a sacramental ordination, which gives the recipient a power of sanctifying (*potestas ordinis*), and on the other by a transmission of pastoral authority (*potestas jurisdictionis*), which at least in its *entire* free and immediate disposability is neither yet granted nor needs to be granted through episcopal consecration. And yet, in the light of what has just been said, these two powers (and the offices held because of them and exercised in them) have an inner unity and an ultimately indissoluble association. If we want to see this, we must not look merely or primarily at the individual bishop as such, but must reflect on the episcopal college as such and on its ontological and logical equality or priority of rank in relation to the individual bishops or to the aggregate of these. Without further ado and without coming into conflict with the fact indicated above,[10] we can thus uphold the thesis that in the episcopal college *as such* a separation between the two powers is impossible. In the first place, the Church cannot be conceived without bishops, that is, without the power of orders—which implies authority over the legitimate celebration of the Eucharist—and that of the normal transmission of this authority (power to ordain). But the Church can also not exist without pastoral authority, for without this the *one* life of the *visible* Church is inconceivable. But it is then also inconceivable that these two powers necessarily existing in the Church are completely and in principle divided between two different holders. For, apart from the question as to how we can even imagine this to be carried out in practice, it is not possible simply because these powers at least partially coincide with one another.

The leader of the celebration of the Eucharist cannot in fact be conceived merely as the person who effects the consecration *ex opere operato*, but as the authoritative leader of the community's celebration with the right and duty of admitting to or excluding from the altar-community as the perfect realization of the unity of the visible Church. But if he does this *because he* is the possessor of this power of *consecration*, then he establishes *ipso facto* sacral law. If the exercise of the sacramental power of reconciliation with God and the

Church in Confession were dependent simply on a person who did not in principle and in every case himself possess this power, then it would be no more than an abstract, theoretical postulate, devoid of reality. The one who imparted jurisdiction for hearing confessions would be the true holder of the Church's power of reconciliation, since he alone would render possible its exercise. This is likewise unthinkable, since this authority implies essentially also authority to admit to the full eucharistic altar-community : something which, from the nature of the case, must belong to the one who leads the community in celebrating the Eucharist. Power of order and pastoral authority therefore at least partially overlap : they are really two factors in one and the same fundamental authority which divides only in relatively secondary operations and applications into two powers, one of which is not of the same character as the other and not determined by the same norms. If in their ultimate roots they are indissolubly connected with one another, then the holder of this one whole power can be he alone who *necessarily* possesses *both*. And this holder is the episcopal college under and with the pope.

It follows therefore that the pope has a duty to receive episcopal consecration, if he is not a bishop when elected. In the matter under consideration we may also justify the ruling of CJC 219 by the fact that as head of the college he already shares in a sense in the power of order of his college, before he himself is ordained as bishop (then also personally sharing in this power, as an individual and not only as a member of

the college); nevertheless, it is more than a requirement of equity and certainly of perspective that the
supreme head of the whole Church, in whom personally the plenitude of pastoral authority resides, should
possess also that power which in the Church and in the
whole college cannot ultimately be separated from
pastoral authority: the power of order in which a holy
right already exists and even originates.[11]

Thus through this unity of powers, in which the one
nature and the one mission of the episcopal college
exist, there can be seen the fact that law and right in
the Church are an expression and a factor of that grace
which is preached in the Gospel: that they are a means
of grace and not an incitement to sin only when they
are borne and redeemed by the grace which is effectively and irrevocably promised to us in the sacraments.

This unity of powers in one and the same holder—
the one episcopal college—suggests from the standpoint of constitutional theology the principle (not
perhaps compelling in every individual case) that when,
with regard to pastoral authority, an "ordinary" holds
his office for life, he particularly ought to be a bishop.
Not only (as we have seen above) because such a person
can appropriately be a member of the supreme directive body of the Church (and vice versa), but also because the exercise of such pastoral authority ought to
be supported by the grace which alone sanctifies power
in the Church, makes it a means of sanctification, and
ought to have—for such decisive events of grace—its
historical and ecclesiological (social) realization in the
sacrament. In the individual case, as we said, this need

not be compelling, because indeed even without such a sacramental foundation and consecration of pastoral authority every ordinary and his actions come within the entirety of the mystical body of Christ and from thence (that is, from the sacrament of Holy Order which exists irrevocably in the Church) this grace is assured also for his actions. Nevertheless, this consideration should be given serious attention in the practice of the Church. The constitutional theological structure of the Church would thereby take on concrete expression more purely and more clearly.

We are naturally not concerned here with the question as to how and why the radically one power of the Church, remaining one in its root, even though possessing two constitutive factors, then still breaks apart into two separate powers which—as bipartite—no longer exhibit precisely the same characteristics. We must note, however, that it is certainly not sufficient to describe the one (power of order) as irrevocable and the other (pastoral authority) as revocable. For in its first holder, the episcopal college with the pope, pastoral authority is likewise irrevocable. The college as such cannot lose it; and the doctrine of the ultimate indefectibility of the Church as such—even constituted as a society—and of the necessity of an historically perceptible, continuous apostolic succession for the power of order and pastoral authority implies that the historically perceptible college with the pope can never (more or less suddenly) cease and be replaced by a college emerging from a *generatio aequivoca*.

The fact of course that Catholic ecclesiology more

or less takes it for granted that a pope is *chosen*—therefore does not receive his office (like the bishop) handed down from his predecessor—and reckons with the possibility of a pope losing his membership of the Church and therefore his office through heresy or schism, shows that the pope's office, rightly understood, is also held by the episcopal college: the election of a new pope is possible because the Church, even on the death (physical or moral) of the pope, remains hierarchically constituted and the office also remains historically present. The Church in such a situation, without a pope, posits an act of supreme importance in canon law—the election of a new pope—even if this act is merely the designation of a person who receives his authority as pope from the Holy Spirit (this is of course only in *one* respect, since the episcopal consecration of the pope is not an event purely "from above" and episcopal authority does indeed belong to the nature of the papacy) and even if the Church is bound to proceed to the act of electing a pope. If then the power of jurisdiction in the Church cannot ultimately be lost, in so far as it rests in the episcopal college, so on the other hand the power of order may be lost in a number of ways or —better—"may be bound", at least as far as rendering an act invalid (for example, the priest's power to absolve, his still radically *sacramentally* conferred power to confirm). It is in fact not yet by any means clear in sacramental theology how far (even if the possibility, for whatever reasons, cannot be unlimited), with regard to a particular holder, the Church may withdraw validity and not only lawfulness from an act even of the power of order. From this point of view we ought to consider afresh the historical questions of "reordinations" in antiquity and the early Middle Ages and of the invalidity of Anglican orders: perhaps the fact is simply that *both* standpoints adopted in these problems are *possible* "in themselves" and that the controversy, properly understood, was really as to whether the Church in her decision *de facto* allowed the validity of a simoniacal ordination (as act) or (from the beginning) withdrew it. (The same might be said of Anglican orders.) From such reflections also we can see how close is the unity of the two powers in the Church. But this is not a question to be pursued further here.

7. *Exemption*

Neither is it possible to consider here the group of problems covered by this catchword to the extent that its true content and scope demand. But, from our basic standpoint, we can certainly gain a very thorough understanding of the properly constitutional theological aspect of the problem.

The episcopal college with and under the pope is one and it has as a college and in its head a function which is intra- or supra-territorial: it is not really made up of the territorially limited functions of its individual members, but is at least put on the same plane as these. But from this basic idea it follows that a person can in principle and appropriately be a member of this college even if he does not at the same time exercise a territorially defined function in the Church, as long at least as his membership of the college is justified on other

57

grounds—as, for example, a cardinal in curia who is a "titular" bishop.

But there are "partial Churches" in the Church which, on the one hand, rightly exist because of the nature of the Church, without being simply a territorial province of the Church, and yet, on the other hand, are of such importance for the whole of the Church and likewise exercise for the Church as a whole precisely the representative function we demanded above for the justification of the territorial diocese in constitutional law. In a word, there are "personal dioceses": at least there can be, and certainly ought to be, in certain circumstances. This does not mean that every "personal diocese" which in fact exists (for example, the military bishopric of Colombia with twenty-four military chaplains) is what it ought to be according to constitutional theology. Just as there are constitutionally legal dwarf-dioceses which from the standpoint of constitutional theology ought not to be, so there may be "personal dioceses" in the same situation.

There may, however, well be large organizations of the Church, representing the whole Church, which do not arise simply through the territorial division of the earth as the one sphere of the Church. For, on the one hand, local attachment is a very important and natural existential of man; but it is not the only one and not necessarily the sole, fundamental consideration when it is a question of the effect of such existentials on the way in which a person enters into the supernatural community of faith, cult and life in the Church. Localization of course is not primarily a specifically Christian and ecclesiastical datum. Its importance for the form of membership in the Church has therefore to be proved, not presupposed as self-evident, particularly since no one today can any longer say that the *necessary* localization of an *altar*-community is itself also identical with the territorial nature of the diocese (as in practice was almost universal in the first centuries of the Church). The territorial principle is one that is appropriate to the nature of a diocese, rightly effective in most cases, but not always the sole valid principle. That is so with the parish; in principle, it is no different with the diocese.

Where there exists a partial group with a representative character for the whole Church, because of the natural conditions of its organization or special ecclesiological peculiarities, which cannot live its own life and reveal its nature within the scope of a territorial diocese, it has in principle the same function and the same right as a territorial diocese. In accordance with existing law, it will then generally have an "ordinary". It takes nothing away then from the territorial diocese : its equally original right is not an exceptional possession of something which in itself should belong solely to a territorial diocese.

The word "exemption" is historically conditioned (because such personal dioceses mostly appeared after the territorial dioceses, it was felt that the juridical recognition of their proper right was an "exception", an "exemption"), but unfortunate; it obscures the real state of affairs. In order to explain exemption as it actually occurs in the Church, it is not sufficient *merely* to appeal to the episcopal and immediate jurisdiction of the pope over every bishop, every diocese and every individual Christian, able thus to place certain members of the Church "directly" under himself. This explanation shows indeed why such "exempt" organizations of the Church always have an episcopal head and are therefore not outside the hierarchical scheme, even if their immediate ordinary is not a local bishop. But in fact "exemption" is an unfortunate expression for immediate subordination to the Apostolic See, since on the one hand the pope exercises an "immediate" jurisdiction over *every* member of the Church and on the other, even when there is an exemption, the pope is not the immediate ordinary. Furthermore, this kind of justification presupposes something which itself has to be justified: namely, that the pope can exercise his *always* immediate jurisdiction in *some* cases even after the abrogation of the existing, territorially structured jurisdiction of an immediate episcopal ordinary and that it is appropriate for him to do so.

We cannot here present individually the organizations similar to a diocese but more personal in structure which, because their nature is similar to that of a true diocese (unity, size, capacity to represent the Church by their own spiritual-ecclesiastical physiognomy), have precisely a "right" (in the wider sense of what ought to be according to constitutional theology) to exist exactly like dioceses—that is, to be under an ordinary of their own. But there are such member-Churches: they are conceivable in the light of constitutional theology and do in fact exist. An "exemption" does not "release" them from their association with the diocese in order to exist, but merely recognizes in constitutional law what already existed as justified by constitutional theology : a member-Church the terrain of which is not the principle distinguishing it from others.

The fact that such organizations have indeed an ordinary in the Church, but mostly not an episcopal ordinary, in no way affects the soundness of these reflections. There are also "partial Churches", apart from such "exemptions", which do not yet have a bishop (for example, apostolic prefectures), but are tending towards such a status. Moreover, it would be best from the point of view of constitutional theology for such "exempt" partial Churches (under the necessary conditions) to have a superior who is a bishop.[12] But we have already said enough about this in another context. If there are rightly such partial Churches which do not really fit in with the territorial principle, nevertheless between them and the local dioceses (as with these among themselves) there ought to be a legally regulated co-operation; and thus the "exemption", in relation to the bishop, can never be absolute. The degree of independence from and indebtedness towards local dioceses naturally varies according to the objective sphere which is involved (inner life, special functions which are not—or not exclusively—the concern of the local bishop, normal pastoral care for the members of a local diocese, and so on). From this standpoint, we might frankly raise the question as to whether these non-episcopal ordinaries who have or really ought to have with equal right a seat at the Ecumenical Council ought not also appropriately to be members of the corresponding episcopal conference.

After these reflections, it is clearly possible to raise a question from the ecumenical standpoint. In order to promote the unity of Christians, might we not more courageously and frankly reckon with the possibility of historically mature Churches, which are still separated but important because of their own history, constitution, liturgy, theology and so on, maintaining to a large extent, in the event of union—under the necessary dogmatic and constitutional-legal conditions—with the Catholic Church, their previous independence and special character, even if they co-exist in the same area as Latin Churches? That may seem impractical and difficult to the merely administrative jurist. But it is no reason for simply levelling down such partial Churches.

8. *The bishop's functions*

If a bishop is *aeque principaliter* both member of the episcopal college and pastor of his own diocese, then it follows that he has duties and responsibilities in regard to the whole Church. He undertakes these indeed *partly* where and in so far as he co-operates as a *member* of the college in a properly collegial act of the college or where and in so far as he simply rules his own diocese and makes it a living member of the whole Church, really contributing to the salvation of the mystical body as a whole. But, because he is a member of the college, he has in addition also as an individual a responsibility for the whole Church (even though, as an individual, he naturally has no pastoral authority in the ordinary sense of the word outside his own diocese), a responsibility for the neighbouring diocese, for the mission of the whole Church and so on. We have explained elsewhere how a co-responsibility of this kind can find institutional expression, for example, in episcopal conferences. This responsibility of each bishop for the whole Church came clearly into action and expression in the constitutional life of the early Church, and indeed already at a time when there was still no sign of a written law on synods or similar institutions through which the individual bishop exercised his responsibility for the whole Church.

9. *The concept of the patriarchate*

If a bishop can be bishop of his diocese solely by being simultaneously a member of the college, then his union and the extent of his co-operation with the other bishops is in principle not a matter which he can decide for himself, but something which flows essentially from the nature of his office. If there is and must be a college, then the union of an individual bishop with the rest of the bishops is not merely the union of all the individual bishops with the pope. This is indeed *one* constitutive factor of the unity of the college—its basis, its guarantee and a criterion of its existence—but not the sole constitutive factor. For the mere unity of many with one still does not make a college out of the many. Such a collegial unity took concrete form in earlier times in the patriarchates : [13] an area that formed geographically, historically and in Church history (in missionary enterprise) a unity, although consisting of several dioceses, became a unity in constitutional law; in other words, the individual sees themselves arose as daughter-Churches from the original unity and were maintained in this unity.

From the viewpoint of constitutional law, we can of course say that these patriarchates are merely of human, ecclesiastical law. But, as suggested above, we must distinguish in the Church two types of human law : a human law which—albeit for sound, objective reasons—comes to divine law more or less purely as an addition, at best as a supplementary aid to divine law and its execution, and that human law which is the concrete expression of divine law. With the latter it may occasionally be very difficult indeed to say where the exact frontier can be drawn between what remains of divine law and its historical, concrete realization. We see this in the bishoprics themselves : each is a concrete realization of the episcopal principle in the Church; taken together, they cannot cease to exist; but no individual diocese can claim that its existence, its frontiers and the precise content of its laws are of divine right.

The ancient patriarchal constitution—even apart from the historical rights of individual existing patriarchates—belongs undoubtedly so closely to the second type of human law in the Church that we might even wonder (if we look at the reality and not merely the nomenclature) whether a patriarchate is less of divine law than a particular diocese or even "the" diocese, that is, the structure in the Church to which this name has in fact been given. We need only recall that, without altering the reality, we could perhaps objectively and terminologically just as well say, instead of "patriarch", "bishop of a large diocese", and regard the bishops under him as auxiliary bishops with the rights of a vicar-general of the (head-) bishop: then we can see that to distinguish between bishop and patriarch as between a matter of divine law and that of human law is by no means so obvious as we usually think.

As soon as we are clear about the collegiality of all bishops, what seems at first sight disturbing about these conditions of fluid transition between the individual juridical structures disappears: ultimately, it is possible to share in the one authority of the one college in various ways which may be determined in the concrete by the Church herself. What the different holders of the different realizable forms of this participation are called, is then almost wholly a matter of terminology— to be made as clear as possible. We can also say quite safely, as long as this is properly understood: the real constitutional-theological nature of the patriarchate belongs to divine law[14] in the Church, because it follows from the collegiality of the bishops that they are bound to realize a concrete, particular union with one another where and when a large, partial Church, embracing several dioceses, has been formed historically, by Church history, sociologically and so on, or when it already existed before the division into these dioceses.

Whether we call such large Churches patriarchates,

metropolitan groups, or anything else, is a secondary question. All the more so since the frontier between the functions and powers of a "patriarch" on the one hand and those of an individual local bishop on the other is fluid and can vary with time and place. Where national, powerful, juridically competent episcopal conferences exist or are in process of being formed, there, objectively speaking, a "patriarchate" already exists, provided that one condition is observed: that there also corresponds to the national (or continental) union of such an episcopal group a large Church which has historically, liturgically (or paraliturgically), theologically and so on, a physiognomy of its own, qualifying it to fulfil a function peculiar to itself (not the same as juridically special) in the whole of the Church.

But if it can be seen clearly that such patriarchates (in many respects newly constructed) exist, or are emerging, paracanonically, then a deliberate effort should be made to ensure that their constitutional-theological nature is clearly reflected in their actual structure. This will include above all a balanced relationship between the patriarch (the title is irrelevant: metropolitan, patriarch, chairman of the episcopal conference, cardinal,[15] or anything else) and the college of the bishops who belong to this "patriarchate". This relationship need not be the same as that which used to exist in the historical patriarchates, still less that which exists *jure divino* between pope and bishops. Precisely because the unity of the episcopate is already guaranteed in the pope, the relationship between the members of the individual episcopal group can be more "democratic". This again does not mean that it is desirable from the point of view of constitutional theology for the "patriarch" in patriarchal law to be *merely primus inter pares*. Since in actual fact, anyway, he will not be such, it is much wiser to recognize this frankly and to make it into a legal datum. There is a greater chance, if this is done, that the "patriarch" will protect rather than reduce the independence and responsibility of the individual bishop, than if he exercises only paracanonically a power which he certainly possesses but which in law has no foundation whatsoever.

10. *An episcopal advisory body to the pope*

It is well known that Paul VI has expressed his willingness—if the Council were to suggest it—to appoint an advisory body, drawn from the bishops of the world, to support him in the government of the universal Church in Rome. In regard to this possibility, from the standpoint of constitutional theology, three points may be made.

1. Such a body is of its nature *advisory*. It cannot restrict the supreme authority of the pope, since this is not dependent on its co-operation. The pope could indeed, if he wanted, work with it as if it were a Council. In the abstract, this body could certainly be conceived as the real and authorized representative of the whole episcopate, so that the pope could make of it a real, permanent Ecumenical Council on a small scale, without its having to consist of very many members. For there have been a number of Councils at which a small

percentage of the total episcopate was present and which still counted as Ecumenical. Moreover, the ecumenicity of very many ancient Councils was a very paracanonical affair : that is, it was due not so much to the nature of the assembly itself as to an express or tacit subsequent assent of the whole episcopate and of the pope. But, as we said, this body is not envisaged as anything more than an advisory one and so we need not think of it as more. Nevertheless it can still have great importance.

2. We must not forget that, even *without* such a body, the constitutional-theological necessity of co-operation between the pope and the whole episcopate can be realized and was and is realized. The *ex sese* of the definition of the First Vatican Council means indeed that the supreme decision of the pope in matters of faith and canon law cannot be subject to any juristic examination or to confirmation by another court of appeal : nevertheless, it does not exclude but includes the fact that the pope thereby acts as head and member of the Church and therefore (since her constitution is essentially episcopal) also as head of the episcopal college; that he is bound by Scripture and the faith of the Church, which has its authentic teaching office in the whole episcopate; that he must proceed according to the norms of justice and charity and therefore must have respect for the Church in her concrete form, in her desires and in her impulses from the Holy Spirit.[16]

A real, living and actual association with the whole episcopate is therefore necessary and self-evident for the pope in every exercise of his office, even though the fulfilment of this necessity is not subject to the legal control of the rest of the bishops, as a false Gallicanism and Episcopalism taught, placing the Council above the pope. Such a unity has also always existed in fact— corresponding to the possibilities and necessities of the time—at least in an adequate (which does not necessarily mean ideal) fashion, even if it was largely realized paracanonically. The bishops are directly or indirectly (through nuncios, etc.) in union with the pope; papal theologians are supported or influenced (reflexively or unreflexively) by the theology of the whole Church, again in contact with the bishops: Rome simply cannot, even if it wanted to, withdraw itself from the influence of the whole life of the Church. Whatever it may be in other respects, in regard to the history of ideas the very fact of saying "No" to a particular trend brings it again under the law of that to which its condemnation was directed. The Church and her Spirit have a thousand ways of influencing Rome and those ways that are not covered by law and therefore not reflexively controlled are perhaps the most effective; but much patience may well be needed until they have worked themselves out and made themselves at home in Rome, in order to re-emerge as impulses from the Church's central government.

Even if the unity of the pope with the whole episcopate, necessary in the light of constitutional theology, is always (*quoad substantiam*) present, it can still be greater or lesser, more rapidly or more slowly effective; it can at different times produce different means and forms of its efficacy, can become more explicitly and canonically comprehensible. And in this respect, from the standpoint of constitutional theology, the planned consultative body is an important and useful institution. It prevents a false perspective, the impression that the life-streams of the Church ran merely from the head to the members, as if the supreme, officially constituted government of the Church were always also the sole point at which the Spirit of the Church could enter with his new charismatic impulses. Thus it can better take account of the present time. For today it is in practice scarcely possible to make sure that the ruler of a large community (society) with manifold tasks in extremely complicated conditions is well-informed unless he is aided by a team-government, brains-trust, or something of the kind, even if he alone has the last word. The idea that, even today, a well-educated man with good intentions and great personal "experience" can be sufficiently well-informed without more ado and without the need of institutionalized information facilities, is old Frankish paternalism which has nothing to do with the juridical freedom and independence of a supreme ruler. Such an advisory body of the world-episcopate around the pope is a good constitutional-legal concrete expression of the constitutional-theological unity of pope and episcopate in the government of the Church. We then see also *where* the responsibility for such information lies; national one-sidedness is more easily avoided; the information can more rapidly and more uniformly be made known.

Naturally, this body must be properly constructed and organized if it is to fulfil its task. It ought in fact to help precisely in overcoming the casual and subjectively conditioned experience of individuals (of the pope and the Roman Curia). This however would not occur if a number of bishops were merely to come together from time to time in Rome for an "informative exchange of ideas". To amass detailed and exhaustive information from all sides requires today—as otherwise in politics at the highest level—organs for the collection, sifting and correct interpretation of events, tendencies, and the emergence of new ideas.

3. From the standpoint at which we are considering this advisory body, it is understandable that those belonging to it must not be *only* non-Roman members of the world-episcopate. If we start out from the principle of constitutional theology that the whole episcopate must not be made up only of diocesan bishops, but can also appropriately have other members, and that—for example—really leading figures of the Roman central government under the pope would have a proper place —according to constitutional theology—in the supreme episcopal directive body, then this would hold also of a kind of "committee" of this episcopal college. If the rector of a university in any way representative of Catholic scholarship is rightly a bishop, then he can perhaps also rightly be a member of this advisory body. The same holds particularly for the episcopal members of the Roman Curia. It is inevitable, but natural, that with the existence of such a body the Roman congregations should appear more than in the past to be merely administrative rather than legislative organs of the pope; but the observance of the principle mentioned

would make it easier to avoid the impression that these congregations with their experience were to be excluded from the deliberations when the episcopal advisory body is engaged in the discussion and making of laws—that is, in the legislature.

Notes

1. If we look at the matter soberly, it is absurd that the superior of a small monastic congregation is a member of the Council while a Franciscan provincial with ten times as many priests under him as many a bishop is not. Is the difference in the length of office (for life or for a limited period) a really adequate justification?

2. This consideration is in no way affected by the fact that other useful things can also be done (parish-visitation, etc.) on such "confirmation-journeys".

3. There are ten auxiliary bishops in the archdiocese of New York.

4. We may here briefly refer to the following point. Just as baptism constitutes a certain, although not complete, membership of the Church, if the baptized person is a heretic or schismatic, so also a valid ordination as bishop confers a certain, although not complete, membership of the episcopal college, if the person ordained is a heretic or schismatic. All the more so if the heresy or schism is merely material and the absence of the *affectus haereticalis aut schismaticus* is sociologically clear.

5. If we recall on the one hand the fact that, under certain conditions, a simple priest can also confirm and indeed even ordain to the priesthood (DS 1145f.), and on the other that, at a normal episcopal consecration, there is in fact always a patriarch or metropolitan taking part as a consecrator, we can see how difficult it is to say dogmatically just what is a bishop. Even if we insist that he is also in fact distinguished from the simple priest *ratione ordinis*, the question still remains open as to whether *this* distinction itself is of divine law, *how* it can be more precisely explained (whether because the simple priest has episcopal power of order, while his acts may be invalidated, or because he simply does not possess it)

and whether it must be the same at all times in the Church or whether the Church's intention in regard to the two orders might itself undergo an historical transformation. It is difficult to define a bishop from the standpoint of the power of jurisdiction, because at least *de facto* his pastoral authority is limited by that of the pope (and possibly other superior bishops) and because even non-bishops can share in the most varied ways in this divisible and measurable power. It really would be therefore clearest and simplest to say, "a bishop is a member of the supreme directive body of the Church", and then to determine *from this fact* what office and what powers he must hold in order appropriately to be called a bishop—that is, from the nature of the case, realistic and appropriate for him to be co-opted into this supreme college.

6. If someone were simply to raise the objection, "But such a person also is still a consecrated bishop", then we need only observe that what we are asking here is precisely, "Who *ought* to be consecrated bishop and under what conditions so that he is appropriately a member of the college governing the whole Church," not whether someone when consecrated is rightly a member of this college.

7. Even if it is not really defined, it is still theologically certain that the triple grade of office (bishop-priest-deacon) belongs to the irrevocable, "divine" constitutional law of the Church. But if we were to think of the priest in this respect merely as an individual, existing simply and solely to the extent that the bishop needs an auxiliary, then we might think of a bishop noticing that he could do without this assistance and in this way tacitly removing the triple grade. It is only necessary to think of the abstract possibility of consecrating every parish priest as bishop and thus of rendering superfluous the assistance of priests as individuals. If then the second grade of the priestly office is really to be *juris divini*, it can be conceived properly only as a college for the bishop : priests do not properly and primarily replace the bishop where he is not, but as a presbyterium support the bishop where he is.

8. Even if an individual consecrated bishop could be conceived in the abstract without priests of his own, he remains nevertheless surrounded by priests as a result of his necessary unity with the whole episcopal college, since the episcopate as a whole can certainly not be conceived without a presbyterium (DS 1776).

9. From the theological standpoint, we must seriously reckon with such a possibility. A partial share in the office of a society, ultimately one because of the unity of the society and of its end and aim, is mutable from the nature of the case and the varying historical situations, without the nature of the one office being thereby changed. There is no evidence that this could not be the case also in the Church. The one office *juris divini* and its three grades of membership need not for that reason be affected. If, for example, one day the Church were to declare that a priest would be in every case and in all circumstances incapable of ordaining other priests, this need not have been the situation always and at all times. The case may be similar with regard to the validity or otherwise of an episcopal consecration without previous ordination to the priesthood. We certainly have an analogous case in the "matter" of the sacrament of Holy Order, the Church expressly leaving open the question as to whether the essential matter was the same at all times (DS 3858–9). Presumably the Church can choose to determine—perhaps by a very unreflexive intention— the extent of the powers she wishes to grant in priestly ordination and thereby also to vary the distance between simple priesthood and episcopal office. A consideration of this kind might perhaps render less formidable some of the historical difficulties in regard to such questions from the early age of the Church.

10. That someone has "episcopal" jurisdiction without being consecrated bishop or that someone is a consecrated bishop without— apparently at least—having the power of jurisdiction.

11. At this point we may be permitted to wonder why it is thought so obvious that the conferring of supreme pastoral authority in the pope is not a grade of the sacrament of Holy Order. It is clear that the *manner* of appointment to office (without imposition of hands) is not an absolute obstacle to its sacramental nature: a sacrament (for instance, Penance and Matrimony) is not necessarily tied to a "matter" distinct from the form (the word promising grace). If we say that the election of a pope (together with acceptance) does not confer a higher power of order, but merely constitutes *ratione jurisdictionis* a higher grade of the hierarchy of office, then the counter-question is justified as to whether this answer—in view of the radical unity of the two powers—is as clear as it seems to be: whether it was not with the aid of an argument similar in form that St Thomas and the theologians of the Middle Ages disputed the sacramentality of episcopal consecration (because, namely, it

confers no new authority—here, in regard to the Body of Christ); whether it is *a priori* certain that the transmission of a power of office is a sacrament—that is, can be linked *ex opere operato* with the conferring of the grace of office—only if this power of office is itself in turn an appointment to sacramental acts.

If we say that the idea of appointment to the papacy as the supreme grade of the sacrament of Order was hitherto unheard of, then it might be pointed out that until the Second Vatican Council it was not absolutely certain that episcopal consecration was a grade of the one sacramental order. It might also be asked whether, in view of the Church's nature as the primordial sacrament, the appointment to the supreme and decisive office in the Church is also the divine, absolute promise of the Spirit of God for the right fulfilment of this office (no matter whether the person wholly accepts this promise or not) and how such an absolute promise is really to be distinguished from an *opus operatum*. It might be asked whether the radical unity of the two powers in the Church does not imply that the gradation of each of the two powers exists on both sides in the same way.

If someone were to object that the appointment as pope does not effect an "inextinguishable mark", the character, which belongs to the essence of the sacrament of Holy Order, it might be pointed out that a pope can be released from his authority only by his own resignation : this is not the case in any other grade of the hierarchy of jurisdiction and therefore by that very fact his office—in that it cannot be lost—is similar to the power of order in the lower grades of the hierarchy of order, particularly since the holders of all these grades can in fact renounce any exercise of their powers; thus the distinction that still remains can be explained from the nature of the case, that is, from the nature of the supreme office which no one can again take upon himself when once he has in principle renounced its exercise.

We must also always remember that the pope is understood in his theological status only if he is seen *also* as bishop, because head of the episcopal college as of the hierarchy of order : thus his appointment as pope necessarily implies a modification of the episcopal authority which he has or ought to have. Why should not this modification in fact have a sacramental character? Merely because we are accustomed to looking at things in this way? But can we not see it in this way if we become used to regarding first of all the grant of office in the Church (as a whole) under the necessary conditions and with the corresponding intention of the Church (to grant a definitive office) as a sacrament and *therefore* and thereby the *gradations* of this grant of office, undertaken by the Church (if perhaps also after apostolic times and irrevocably), as sacramental grades of the one sacramentally bestowed office?

12. We must not forget: at the very moment at which the life of the evangelical counsels is given institutional form in an Order expressly controlled by the Church, it is no longer possible to say that the consecration of its ordinary as bishop in order to bring this institution into the hierarchy is contrary to the spirit of such a life of the free charisms as the religious life does indeed try to be.

13. We are not concerned here with the distinction between patriarchs and metropolitans, which is historically conditioned and objectively fluid if we look beyond the words to the thing itself. All that we are saying here might be brought also under the titles of "head-bishop" and "head-diocese".

14. In which it is implied that this *jus divinum* must become concrete in particular historical forms and rightly finds *different* concrete expressions according to time and place.

15. If the structure of the college of cardinals is such as we sketched above, if—in other words—the college of cardinals truly represents the whole episcopate (which of course does not mean that it must be made up *merely* of residential bishops), and when consequently in many cases (not necessarily always and exclusively) cardinals and presidents of national conferences are practically identical, then "Cardinal" might well be the new title for the person who according to constitutional theology is what is meant by a real patriarch. This would also provide an opportunity of getting rid of the tiresome question of the relationship between patriarchs and cardinals. In the face of such a development it would be possible to get away even more boldly than did John XXIII from the traditional number of seventy cardinals. Of the forty-four episcopal conferences listed in the *Annuario Pontificio* a great number would qualify to have a cardinal as president, or already have one. From that standpoint alone we must not think meanly of the college of cardinals, since it cannot be conceived as composed only of the presidents of episcopal conferences.

16. This is so true that the old canonists openly reckoned with the possibility that the pope, if he did not act in this way and

therefore became a heretic or at least a schismatic (through *his* separation from the whole organism of the Church), ceased to be a Catholic and thus also ceased to be pope.

CHALLENGE BOOKS

form a new series in the Paperbooks published by Helicon
Press. Written with the seriousness and depth demanded
by their subjects, they are concerned with the latest
developments in theology, biblical studies, liturgy, and
the situation of the Church in the modern world. They
are intended to provide an opportunity, through pertinent
analysis and discussion, for re-evaluating and rediscover-
ing the meaning of the Christian message in our time.

IN THE BEGINNING . . .: Genesis I-III

JEAN DANIELOU (*Preface by Gerard S. Sloyan*)

Father Danielou removes Genesis from being the stumb-
ling-block to modern scientific minds, facing squarely
all the problems created by a scientific interpretation of
Genesis. A careful examination of Genesis introduces us
to the universal scope of salvation history: Adam as the
first man, whose failure is to be transformed into
victory by the first man of the new race, Christ; and the
seventy peoples identified in Genesis as symbolizing all
peoples and expressing the fundamental solidarity of all
men as well as their common involvement in God's plan.

$1.25

HELICON PAPERBOOKS

THE PILL—AND BIRTH REGULATION

LEO PYLE, editor

The final solution to "the problem of The Pill" is a complicated issue. It involves many factors which include the population explosion, the nature and precise method of applying the principles of the natural law, the problem of authority and infallibility in the Church, the value of the layman's knowledge and experience, the real meaning of marriage and the sacrament of matrimony. In this book, Cardinal Ottaviani, Archbishop Roberts, Bishop Bekkers, Canon Janssens, Father Francoeur, Father Bernard Haring, Michael de la Bedoyere, among others, cast light on what the Church's ultimate position will be.

$1.65

PREPARING FOR MARRIAGE

JOHN MARSHALL, M.D.

The requirements for a successful union between two people in a marriage are: common sense, correct values— and a touch of humor. These are the qualities which Dr. Marshall brings to this practical, simply written, easy-to-read and *authoritative* introduction to marriage. He discusses the physical aspect of love, anatomy and physiology, contraception, the purpose of marriage, love, understanding one another, courtship—and even budgeting!

$1.25